RUTLEDGE HILL PRESS®
NASHVILLE, TENNESSEE

TELEPHONE (XXX) XXX-XXX

DEA REG. NO. XX xxxxx

TO

ADDRESS

DATE

℞

live like you were dying

☐ LABEL

REFILL _____ TIMES

M.D.

M.D.

DISPENSE AS WRITTEN

MAY SUBSTITUTE

foreword by T I M   M c G R A W

live
like you were dying

TIM NICHOLS AND CRAIG WISEMAN

RUTLEDGE HILL PRESS® • NASHVILLE, TENNESSEE

A DIVISION OF THOMAS NELSON, INC.

From the second we began writing "Live Like You Were Dying," the song took over. We talked on the phone at midnight to finish the second verse because the song would not wait. Tim McGraw said it would be the first song on his next record. He never blinked. He made an amazing recording and stayed true to the song.

All along, "Live Like You Were Dying" has had a destiny, a soul of its own, and we have simply had the honor to write it down and stay out of the way as it took us on an incredible journey. This song told us it was a book that we would write long before we wondered if we knew how to write a book or who would publish it. But this song opened those doors, too, and spoke to us as we wrote these pages.

And now, here you are holding this book. Coincidence? Happenstance? Possibly.

Or maybe this book has come to you right when you needed it most and now it is time for your life to be touched by this song as it has touched ours.

God bless,

Tim Nichols and **Craig Wiseman**

Live Like You Were Dying

He said, "I was in my early forties, with a lot of life before me,
When a moment came that stopped me on a dime.
And I spent most of the next days looking at the x-rays
And talking 'bout the options, talking 'bout sweet time."

And I asked him when it sank in
That this might really be the real end.
"How's it hit you when you get that kind of news?
Man, what'd you do?" He said,

"I went sky diving; I went rocky mountain climbing;
I went two point seven seconds on a bull named Fumanchu.
And I loved deeper, and I spoke sweeter,
And I gave forgiveness I'd been denying."
And he said, "One day I hope you get a chance
To live like you were dying."

He said, "I was finally the husband that most the time I wasn't.
And I became a friend a friend would like to have.
And all 'a sudden going fishin' wasn't such an imposition
And I went three times that year I lost my dad.

"And I finally read the good book and I took a good long hard look
At what I'd do if I could do it all again . . . and then

"I went sky diving; I went rocky mountain climbing;
I went two point seven seconds on a bull named Fumanchu.
And I loved deeper, and I spoke sweeter,
And I gave forgiveness I'd been denying."
And he said, "One day I hope you get a chance
To live like you were dying."

Like tomorrow was a gift
And you've got eternity to think of what you did with it . . .
What you did with it . . . What did I do with it?

A lot of people assume that I recorded this song because of the passing of my father, Tug McGraw. But my passion for this song goes a lot further.

I love this song because I believe that everyone who hears it will have their own unique reaction to it. Each person has his or her own definition of what it means to "live like you were dying." That's what makes it such a great song. It's not just about my personal connection—although obviously there is one—it's about how you connect to it.

I hope this song can provide inspiration for all of us to stop and take time to appreciate all the blessings in our lives—from the smallest things to the biggest dreams.

God bless,

Tim McGraw

I care about you.

I've been longing to tell you something. And now is the perfect time.
It's one of the secrets of life.

It's not how to get rich quick, but it will enrich your life.
It isn't the fountain of youth, but it will keep you young at heart.
It probably won't make your life longer, but it will make your life better.

FULLER, DEEPER, BROADER, BETTER.

"LIVE *like you were dying*"

It's simple. The best things always are. I hope it becomes your prayer, your motto, your mantra. I hope it becomes a part of you. Every day.

WE'RE ALL TERMINAL.
Some of us are just lucky enough to know it.

Life is a spiritual journey.
And sometimes all you have to do is show up
and have a little faith that something
completely amazing is possible any day.

And every now and then,
right when you least expect it,
something amazing does happen.

And you are no more in control
than a feather is of the wind.
All you know is that the force moving you is so strong
that you just hang on in wonder.

There is nothing but the moment
and the sense of dancing with angels.

So ALIVE . . .

I know you have big, beautiful, dangerous, exhilarating, far-flung, impossible dreams that you keep tucked away. You think so many things stand in your way of finding those dreams, those hopes, those wishes . . . of finding the YOU that you desire. You think it's too soon, it's too late, it's too hard, it's too crazy . . .

But all of that is about to change. The greatest

journeys begin with a single step. Sometimes that first step is the magical leap a dream takes from the dark, silent depths of your heart to the brilliant light and sound of the spoken word.

Some say that once spoken, a sound never dies. Like ripples on a pond from a tossed stone, it reverberates on and on, back and forth, forever. That sound vibrates, spreads out, touches, finds resonance and harmonies, sets events in motion.

Today, take the first step of the long journey and make your dreams known by giving them voice, substance, reality. After this, neither you nor your world will ever be the same again.

So take a few moments to prepare. Take a deep breath, slowly in, slowly out.

Pick up that smooth, cool stone that has been hidden in your soul for so long and prepare to shatter the still, glassy status quo forever. Now close your eyes and complete the most important sentence you may ever speak. I am . . .

Go! Just Go!
Right, left, wrong, right—Go!
No stopping and looking back. No what-ifs. Just Go!
This is something new.
There are no wrong moves—you'll learn from everything.
There are no mistakes except inaction. Go!
You're scared to do this?
I'm scared you won't do it.
Go, even if it's in the completely wrong direction at first.
Say your prayers and Go!

What are you waiting for? Get a move on!

ONE-WAY TICKETS

"What's the secret of your success?" I asked the old veteran music man. He had been in London with the Beatles, in Los Angeles with the Eagles. He had become rather wealthy and managed to make himself a living legend in the process of constructing an amazing career that spanned the decades and the globe.

"The secret to my success is a lot simpler than you would imagine," he said. "It's one-way tickets."

"What?" I asked.

"One-way tickets," he said. "I went everywhere knowing that I was going to have to make it wherever I landed and that there were no other options."

"You mean you flew off, even out of the country, without enough money to come home?" I asked.

He smiled and said, "Most of the time I didn't have enough for a decent room. But . . ." As he lit an expensive cigar he smiled and said, "It worked out all right."

"*and I Loved* **DEEPER**"

You can't control
the length of your life.
Just the DEPTH.

At some point we all start to realize that the fabulous life and fabulous friends we had always thought we were going to have were not going to happen, and we just have to make do with the incredibly odd assortment we have been given. So the only thing to do is start treating your life and your friends and your time together . . . well . . . fabulously.

I started telling those around me, **I LOVE YOU**

Saying "I love you" is always a little hard at first (especially for guys). But I just took a deep breath and did it. Pretty soon we all got used to it and I began to wonder if it had lost its power.

But then one day something serious happened, and the calls went out and the prayers went up. We were all reminded just how fragile it all can be, how much these relationships mean, how connected we really are.

A friend called for an update and at the end of the conversation, I said, "I Love You." He paused and said, "I Love You, too." And all of the meaning and depth and magic came rushing back stronger than ever.

At that moment I was so glad I had made the effort to lift the intimacy in our little group to the point where it was OK to say the most powerful phrase in the world.

So right now,
BEFORE you turn the page
And get on with your life,
BEFORE another moment passes away,
Let me be the first to say it.

Pass it on.

I LOVE YOU. It's not a weight you must carry around.

I LOVE YOU. It's not a box that holds you in.

I LOVE YOU. It's not a standard you have to bear.

I LOVE YOU. It's not a sacrifice I make.

I LOVE YOU. It's not a pedestal you are frozen upon.

I LOVE YOU. It's not an expectation of perfection.

I LOVE YOU. It's not my life's whole purpose.

I LOVE YOU. It's not your life's whole purpose.

I LOVE YOU. It's not to make you change.

I LOVE YOU. It's not even to make you love me.

I LOVE YOU. It's as pure and simple as that.

I love you.

I'm beginning to suspect
That the moment we have been waiting for
Doesn't require waiting.

And the things we'll remember most
Won't be things at all.

YOU ARE BEAUTIFUL . . .

When you let friends have their space.

When you believe.

When you laugh or are moved to tears.

When you let it just roll right off your back.

When you talk about your dreams.

When you help a turtle across the road.

When you try to do the right thing . . .

   even when it comes out wrong.

You are beautiful when you **LOVE**.

"AND I Spoke SWEETER"

You have the power to change someone's life,
To give a moment that will be cherished forever.
Deeper than deep, higher than high,
A simple honest act can bring meaning and depth and poetry
To someone who needs it more than they know.
Your honest words say you care about . . .
your **friend**, your **family**, your **lover**, your Savior.
Your honest words say you cherish them, that you are better
because of them, and that you would be lesser without them.

So just say it now. Don't wait. You've waited long enough.

Tell a little girl with no front teeth that she is beautiful.

Ask an old man to tell you about the "good old days."

Be a big tipper. It feels good.

Don't fight tears. Let them win.

Just listen to a friend who needs to talk.

Give away something you have held dear.

Tell the little old lady with no front teeth she is beautiful.

Remind
   your loved ones that they are loved,
   your friends that they are the best,
   your family that they are your lifeline,
   yourself that you don't stop and say these things enough.

And a lot of times . . .
   DON'T SAY ANYTHING at all.

Way to go dude!

The house was sold,

     its contents auctioned off,

and the car given to charity.

All that was kept

     were a few LETTERS.

Why do we keep them?

Under our bed, up in the attic, in the back of some drawer. We could have thrown them out a thousand times, and yet there they are . . . still. Old Love Letters. Written to a person we no longer are, by a hand we no longer hold. Sappy cards and faded stationery, old and deeply wrinkled at the creases. Why do we keep them? Maybe because they are the mile markers of our journey, the currency of our soul and our past. They give our lives a value nothing else can even approach. They mark the times in our lives when we knew we were loved.

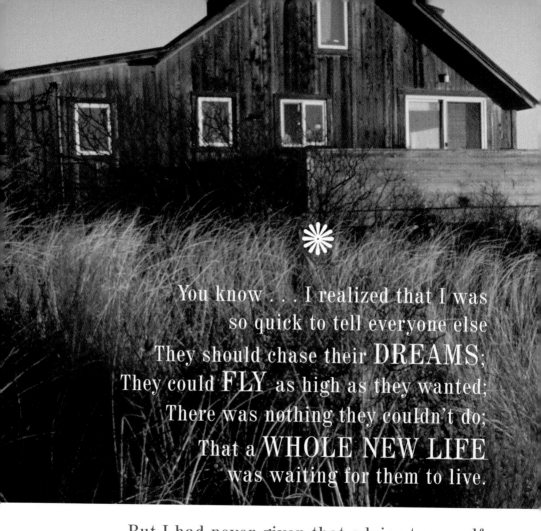

You know . . . I realized that I was
so quick to tell everyone else
They should chase their DREAMS;
They could FLY as high as they wanted;
There was nothing they couldn't do;
That a WHOLE NEW LIFE
was waiting for them to live.

But I had never given that advice to myself . . .

Too many STOP signs.

Maybe that's the problem. There are just too many stop signs in this world. Every road you go down, just when you're about to get somewhere . . . there's another stop sign.

It's a metaphor of our lives that every road has stop signs all over it. It's no wonder so many people feel as if they will never get to their dreams. It's no wonder so many people don't even bother to begin the chase. They know there will be so many stop signs.

Well, I decided to do something about it. I decided to tie a little ribbon around every stop sign between my house and where I go every day just to remind me that while my car or bike should stop frequently, I and my dreams and my journey should not stop.

Those little ribbons remind me that I need to keep going, that I should pursue my dreams, that I shouldn't be standing still. Those little ribbons remind me that stop signs are for cars and buses and motorcycles. Stop signs are not for dreams and hopes and plans and adventures. Because of those little ribbons, the stop signs now remind me to . . . GO!

Dearest One,

Let me tell you how very proud I am of you. The doubts you had makes your passing the exams for business with such flying colors all the more amazing. I hope you realize how much you can accomplish when you set your mind to it. You are stronger than you realize. You can rise to your challenges. You are such an inspiration!

When you feel like you're alone, know that I'm always in your corner, cheering you on. You are always in my prayers. God bless you.

I love you very, very much.

Aunt Milly

"I used to have an Aunt Milly," a friend told me as emotion filled his eyes. "She was incredible. All she ever said were things like 'You can do it,' 'You're so talented, I believe in you' 'You're strong enough,' and 'You're going to be great.'"

"I can't remember a single time she ever said anything negative. At every birthday, graduation, and major event in my life, Aunt Milly was there, cheering me on, encouraging, loving.

"It forever changed me. She has been and will forever be that whisper in my heart that tells me . . . I can when I think I can't, that I am more than I think I am and better than I thought I was."

"What a beautiful, beautiful soul. I wish everyone could have an Aunt Milly in their lives."

Your number's up, the STARS align.
Tomorrow is the day.
Who will hear you speak those words
That you've kept locked away?

A stranger or a long-lost friend,
An enemy no more.
A son, a father, mother, daughter,
Husband, or a wife.
Perhaps the one who sends the prayer
That heaven spare your LIFE.

NORTH STAR

BIG DIPPER

"and I gave
FORGIVENESS
I'd been denying"

FORGIVE . . . FORGET

FOR LIFE
FOR LOVE
FOREVER

AMEN!

Hey, would you do me a favor?

Just let it go.

I know how long you've carried it around and how heavy it is.

Just let it go.

Deep down, you know it was just one of those things.

Just let it go.

You've had it so long, it's hard to imagine life without it.

Just let it go.

You know we weren't made to hang on to it.

Just let it go.

Right now. This moment. You've waited long enough.

Just let it go.

Take all of that forgiveness locked up deep inside you and . . .

Just let it go.

And then you can give the **forgiveness** you've been denying.

Oh, yeah,

Just one more thing . . .

Forgive
yourself.

Do something that makes your heart
beat **faster** every day.

Give the dog a bite of your sandwich.

Play air guitar—rock 'n' roll air guitar.

If it's short, let it grow . . . You can always cut it.

If it's long, cut it . . . You can always let it grow.

Don't underestimate the power of a crayon.

Wear pajamas out for the evening.

Top down. Radio up. Laughing friends.

Laugh until you cry. And vice versa.

"What's the secret to success?" I asked.

"Two words," he said.

"Right decisions."

"How do you make right decisions?"

"One word," he said.

"Experience."

"And how do you get experience?"

"Two words," he answered.

"Wrong decisions."

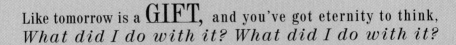

Like tomorrow is a GIFT, and you've got eternity to think, *What did I do with it? What did I do with it?*

This is my prayer for me, for you, for my friends, for Loretta Lynn and . . . OK . . . even for my enemies. My prayer for that guy who was yelling at the cashier in the grocery store, for a kid starting college, and for that woman who just found a lump. My prayer for my dog Pester, for that old man who always walks by my house every afternoon talking to himself, and for anyone who believes. And this is my prayer especially for you if you don't believe in coincidences and that this little book came into your life right when you needed it . . . This is my prayer for all of us.

May we live like we were dying.
With passion and purpose and mission and meaning . . .
and with a little wild abandon. With no forgiveness
withheld and no anger held within.

MAY WE LIVE LIKE WE WERE DYING.

With a heart full of memories,
precious and true,
like a Bible that we can open anywhere
and find ourselves and faith.
With friends and family and hugs
and laughter and singing and praying
and crying and holding hands and
saying all the sappy stuff.

Then and only then . . .

may we
die like
we were
living

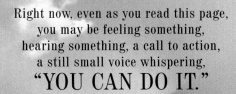

Right now, even as you read this page,
you may be feeling something,
hearing something, a call to action,
a still small voice whispering,
"YOU CAN DO IT."

You have everything
you need already inside you.
You have spirit that has never been tested,
muscles you have never used.
It's all there waiting . . .
**MAY YOU LIVE LIKE
YOU WERE DYING.**